I0213300

GOD'S GENERALS

FOR KIDS

A. A. ALLEN

GOD'S GENERALS
FOR KIDS

A. A. ALLEN

BY
ROBERTS LIARDON
& OLLY GOLDENBERG

BRIDGE
LOGOS

Newberry, FL 32669

Bridge-Logos
Newberry, Florida 32669 USA

God's Generals For Kids—A. A. Allen
Roberts Liardon & Olly Goldenberg

Copyright ©2020 Roberts Liardon & Olly Goldenberg

All rights reserved. Under International Copyright Law, no part of this publication may be reproduced, stored, or transmitted by any means—electronic, mechanical, photographic (photocopy), recording, or otherwise—without written permission from the Publisher.

Library of Congress Catalog Card Number 2018903567

International Standard Book Number 978-1-61036-211-5

eBook International Standard Book Number 978-0-7684-5845-9

Hardcover International Standard Book Number 978-0-7684-6006-3

Large Print International Standard Book Number 978-0-7684-6007-0

Unless otherwise noted, all Scripture is from the King James Version of the Bible.

The photographs used are owned by and taken from the private collection of Roberts Liardon.

Timeline illustrations by David Parfitt.

A. A. ALLEN

CONTENTS

TIMELINE

1911

March 27 1911 Born in Arkansas

1925 Left home

June 1934 Saved

Sept 19 1936 Married Lexie

1951 July 4 First tent meeting

1953 November First radio programme

1955 Arrested for drink driving

1958 Miracle Valley is bought

1967 Separates from wife

June 11 1970 Dies

1925

1934

1951

1936

1953

1955

1970

1958

1967

CHAPTER 1

BORN DRUNK

Asa A. Allen

A TORTURED CHILDHOOD

It's horrible when people laugh at you.

If it happens to you lots, it can change your life. People who are bullied can feel scared. After a bit they just push it away hoping it will go away. If they are made to do dangerous things they often dream of being somewhere else.

When your own parents push you into danger then life can be very hard. All day long all you know is fear and you don't have anywhere to go to.

Asa Alonso Allen had lots to be scared of at home. He had six older brothers and sisters. And his father was a drunk.

Asa's dad spent all his money on alcohol. Asa's dad spent all his time drinking. The children had to get on with life.

When Asa's dad had friends round the bullying really started. Asa and the other small children in the house were forced to drink alcohol. The adults wanted to make the children drunk. They wanted to laugh at the children.

The little toddlers would drink so much that they would fall over and not be able to get up. This made the adults laugh even more.

Asa's parents both loved to smoke. Asa could light a cigarette before he knew how to read. It was his job to light his mom's cigarettes. Each time he lit one he would take a few puffs of smoke from it, then give it to his mom.

MY FIRST SHOES

When Asa's parents were not harming him, they did not look after him. He had to look after himself all day. He didn't even own a pair of shoes.

Asa loved to stand next to the road. Every day he watched the horse and cart go by. The cart carried people into town. Little Asa loved to wave at the driver when he went past. The driver always looked at him and waved back.

The cart driver knew that Asa's father was a drunk. The driver could see little Asa never wore shoes. He felt sorry for Asa. One day he stopped his cart right next to Asa.

"Come here boy, I've got something for you."

Asa ran up to the cart and smiled. The driver pulled out a pair of brand new shoes. They were black and red and made of real leather. Asa looked at them.

"Go on, take them. They're yours."

Asa beamed, "Thank you."

He sat down and put the shoes on. They were his very first pair. He felt so special.

No one in his family had ever given him shoes. But this stranger had. Asa loved those shoes so much. He wasn't four years old yet, but he remembered that day for the rest of his life.

When Asa turned four, his little life looked like it was about to get better. His mother had had enough. She did not want to live with Asa's dad anymore. She left him drinking and took the children with her.

For a few months things were a bit better. Then she married again, and her new husband also drank too much.

FETCH ME SOME BEER

Asa's mom and stepdad fought a lot. When they were drunk, they would fight so much that Asa and his sisters were scared. They did not know what would happen. Things would be thrown around the house and the two adults would hit each other.

The children did not feel safe. If they stayed in the same room a flying object would hit them. They knew it was safer outside. So they ran out and stayed away. Several hours later they would creep back into the house. They did not know what they would find. Would the police be there? Would both parents be at home still?

As little children they half expected to come back and find that one of their parents had been killed by the other one. It was a terrifying time.

In this new home the children were still picked on. Asa was made to do things that no child should ever have to do. Sometimes he had to carry a bucket of beer home to his stepfather. It was so heavy. Asa struggled to pick it up. It was even harder to carry it. But he had to get home fast.

If he took too long his stepdad would be angry. If he spilt any beer his stepdad would be even more angry. Asa was so frightened that he always managed to get that bucket home somehow.

I'VE HAD ENOUGH

When Asa was 11 years old he had had enough. He did not want to stay at home another day. He loved his mother, but he couldn't stand his stepfather. Every job he had to do for his stepdad made him feel sick.

Asa had a plan. He was going to run away. He was going to find his real dad.

Asa lay in bed at night waiting for the whole house to be quiet. When everyone was asleep he slipped out of bed and wrote a letter. He carefully put the letter on his pillow and got dressed. His heart was beating fast as he climbed out the window towards his freedom.

Asa knew where his dad lived, but he didn't know how to get there. He knew he had to follow the railway south to get to his dad. He ran through the darkness straight to the railway line and started walking.

He hadn't got very far when he saw a flashlight. Asa wasn't the only person out that night. The railway guard was walking along the line too.

Asa did not want to be caught. If the guard saw him, he would send him home. Asa needed the railway to help him find his dad. But right now he had to avoid the guard. He needed the line if he was to find his dad, but more importantly he needed to stay away from home.

He walked faster, moving away from the railway.

Then the wind started to blow. Dry leaves attacked him as the wind picked them up and threw them in his face. Lightning started to flash around him. Rain began to fall.

Asa had been scared many times before. Now he was so scared that he felt sick. Another flash of lightning lit up the whole area for a short time. Asa looked around but was thrown back into darkness. The wind pushed against him. Still Asa tried to fight on.

He did not want to go back. He had walked for miles. But there were hundreds of miles still to go. Surely he was far enough away from home for now.

He found a ditch and hid in it. The wind howled around him like a wild wolf, but it did not feel so strong in there. The rain was falling but Asa was too tired to care. He snuggled under some leaves and fell asleep.

All through that night the rain kept falling. When Asa woke up he thought he was in the bath. As he opened his eyes it took him a while to remember where he was. The ditch had filled with water. His clothes were soaked.

Asa stood up and started to walk. He wished he had a jumper. He wished he had a coat. The wind blew straight through his wet clothes taking all his warmth and leaving him shivering. Asa had walked a long way for an 11 year old boy. Now he could not go on. He had been beaten by the weather.

Home was horrible. He did not want to go back, but he had no choice. At home they had a roof and walls. At home the wind could not blow through him. At home he had dry clothes.

Unwillingly, Asa turned round. He knew he had to go home. He arrived home in time for lunch. As he ate, he started to plan how he would leave for good. Next time his plans would be better.

CHAPTER 2

TRYING TO BE GROWN UP

A. A. Allen in action

AWAY BUT NOT FREE

When Asa was 14 he decided to run away again. This time he took spare clothes and food with him.

He had grown up a lot in the last few years. Now he was as strong as a grown man. He could do almost anything he was asked to do. He planned to travel around and earn money at the same time. And that's just what he did.

In one place he would pick cotton from the field, in another he would dig ditches. In one town he was a waiter in a restaurant, in another he went to college and learned to be a barber. Asa did so many different jobs and in each job he did well.

But he could not stay still for long.

Life was not pleasant. Sometimes he found a bed to sleep in. Often he ended up sleeping on the street. He went to sleep hungry and woke up feeling ill. When the sun shone he overheated. When it was cold he would shiver.

Life was hard, but it was better than life at home. Asa had learned how to be cheerful no matter how bad things got. He would sing to himself so he could stay smiling and he loved to dance.

When Asa turned up at a party he brought the fun with him. He made people laugh and everyone would start to dance with him.

Then he would have a drink.

Sometimes he would drink so much that he would fight with people, just like his parents had done. He didn't care about himself or others. Each time he ended up in a lot of trouble. If a fight got really bad the police would come and warn Asa. But Asa never changed. Before long they would lock him up in prison.

When they let him out he moved to a new town. In the new town the parties and the fights would start again. In each place it was not long before he was sent to prison again. Asa didn't care. At least in prison he had a bed and was safe from the wind and the rain.

At some parties Asa would drink so much that he would feel ill. The next morning, he would wake up with a headache, feeling sick. "I'm never going to drink again," he would promise himself.

That evening he would be at another party drinking again. He could not keep his promise. Alcohol was his master and he had to obey.

TAKING ON THE FAMILY TRADE

Asa had become just like his father. As a child he was forced to drink. Now he could not stop drinking even if he wanted to. Because of his parents, his whole family was in a mess. He had two brothers. One had died as a child. The other died a drunk. His father died a drunk. Asa's four sisters used to drink loads even as children. It was clear they were all going to end up as drunkards too.

Now Asa was a drunk. He could not live without alcohol. If he did not drink his whole body would shake. The only thing that stopped the shaking was more alcohol. The shakes were so bad that he couldn't even have a drink without spilling it.

"Do you want a coffee, Asa?" his friends would ask.

"Just fill my cup half way."

Even with half a cup Asa had to concentrate. He would grip the cup with both hands and slowly bring it to his mouth. The alcohol was destroying his life. And so were the cigarettes. Asa had been smoking cigarettes before he was five. Now he smoked non-stop.

By the time he was 21 he was always coughing. He tried different types of cigarettes, but he could not get rid of the cough. Whenever he tried to stop his whole body would scream at him until he had a puff of smoke. His body was falling apart.

WHAT'S THE POINT OF LIFE?

It wasn't just his body that wasn't working. His mind was also wearing out. He would get up to do something and forget what he was supposed to do. He struggled to wash and dress. There was no way he could work. What did he have to live for? What was the point of his life?

"If I kill myself this horrible life will be over," Asa thought. He wanted his troubles to end. He knew he could not kill himself.

"People will know that I quit life. I am not a coward, I will not quit."

There was only one thing that Asa could only think to do.

"If I go back home I can work on the farm. At least I will have proper food to eat."

So, Asa set off home. As he walked in through the door his mom wept. She had not seen her son for years. When she last saw him he was strong and fit, just a few years later his life was a total mess. He looked ill and he moved like an old man.

"Asa, please don't follow the rest of the family," his mom begged. "I stopped drinking, I know you can too. It's destroying your life."

"I know it is mom. But this IS my life. It's the only thing I have."

"SAVE HIM, MOVE HIM OR KILL HIM"

Back at home Asa carried on like before.

Every Saturday night he had a big party in his house. Everybody in town knew about it. Loads of people went each week. They loved dancing but they also knew there would be lots of alcohol. Asa didn't have to buy any. He made his own. Every week more people turned up to join him. They thought it was fun.

But one man was not impressed. A short walk away lived a farmer called Brother Hunter. He had met Jesus and been filled with the Holy Spirit. Now he wanted everyone to know God like he did. Every Sunday morning Hunter invited people to come to his home. He ran prayer meetings and church meetings. He wanted to see loads of people saved, but it did not happen.

Sometimes a young person would come and give their life to Jesus. By Saturday night they would be back in Asa's home, no longer interested in God. It seemed like every young person was at the Asa Dance Hall. Nobody wanted to be saved.

Hunter was desperate.

"If we're ever going to win people to God that dance hall has to close," he told his small group of followers. "Let's pray."

And their prayer was very clear:

"Lord, close down that dance hall. Save Allen if you can. But if he doesn't want you then move him out of town or kill him. We don't care which one, but please just close down that dance hall!"

Their prayer was not the most godly prayer in the world. It was a desperate prayer. God doesn't want to kill people and we shouldn't pray for people to be killed! But God knew their hearts. They wanted to see people saved.

God heard their prayer and he answered it.

CHAPTER 3

A NEW CREATION

A. A. Allen praying

ANSWERED PRAYER

"Asa, I've got to do a job. Do you want to come and help?"

It was June 1934. One of Asa's friends was standing at the door.

"Sure, why not?" Asa replied. "I've got nothing better to do."

So Asa and his friend set out on the road. On their way they went past a small Methodist church. The door was open and Asa peered inside. The people were all singing a song and they seemed so happy.

Asa had always thought that church was boring. He thoughts churches were full of serious, boring people. But these people were full of life. Their faces were shining.

Asa and his friend slipped inside and found a seat. It was right behind a huge stove so they could hide from the preacher. After all they didn't want to join the church. They just wanted to see what was happening.

When the preacher stood up Asa was shocked. The preacher was a woman! She was wearing white clothes and had a huge smile.

"She looks like an angel," Asa murmured to himself.

The preacher lady started to talk about the sins people do. Asa hid behind the stove, but she moved so she could see him. Every word that she spoke was about his life. It seemed like she knew him.

Asa moved behind the other side of the stove. The preacher lady moved too. She was looking into his eyes again. Every time she looked at him Asa knew he was a sinner. He had never felt it before, but in that church he discovered the truth. He had blamed his dad for his problems. He had tried to blame the alcohol too. But at that moment he could not escape it. His problem was that HE was a sinner.

It was too much for him to cope with. He had to get out of there. He stood up and ran out of the church before the preacher lady got him saved. He had to get away from that feeling. But the feeling did not leave him. Wherever he went that night he knew he was a sinner. God was convicting him.

For years he had been looking for peace and joy. The people in that church had it. A big fight was going on inside him. Could Jesus really be the answer? Something dark tried to pull him back. God gently nudged him forward.

COMING BACK FOR MORE

The next night Asa had to get to the church of happy people. He arrived before the meeting started. He did not want to miss one bit of it. When the service began it felt like it was just for him. Every song that was sung seemed to be like a hug from God. Every testimony gave him hope.

The preacher lady was there again. She spoke about the blood of Jesus. "It washes away every sin. No sin is too big for the blood of Jesus." She looked around the room and saw Asa. She remembered him from the night before. He was a rough looking man who had scars from his fights.

"He must be here to make trouble," she thought. But she carried on preaching.

"If you want to give your heart to Jesus please lift up your hand." Asa didn't hesitate, his hand shot up in the air.

"If you really want to be saved tonight, stand up." Asa stood. A couple of other people stood with him.

"If you *really* mean business with God come to the front of the church." Only Asa moved. He walked to the front of the church and stood. The preacher waited.

"Why isn't he kneeling," she thought. "Surely he would kneel if he wanted to pray to God!"

Asa waited.

"I've done everything she asked, what's she waiting for?" Asa wondered. The preacher broke the silence.

"Do you *really* want to be saved?"

"That's why I've come here."

"Then please will you kneel." She was shocked when he did. This man was serious. That evening, at the front of a Methodist church, Asa gave his life to Jesus. At that moment Jesus changed him instantly.

ALL CHANGE

No more dances.

No more drinking.

No more smoking.

Asa had changed overnight. For years he had tried to stop the habits that were killing him. Now God had healed him instantly. When his friends heard what had happened, they burst out laughing. "Asa's got religion!"

"It won't last," one teased.

"If it goes on more than a month I might try it too," another mocked.

But they did not know that Asa had really changed. He didn't even sing the songs he used to. He only wanted to sing about Jesus. Jesus really had given him freedom: Freedom from his past and freedom from himself. Now Asa filled his time with God.

"Asa," his mom asked, "can you stop singing these religious songs. You sing them all day long."

But Asa didn't stop. Up in the attic he found a Bible. One of his sisters had been given it when she was a little girl. It had never been opened. Now Asa did not stop reading it. In the morning he came down to breakfast reading the Bible. As he worked in the fields he read the Bible. At night time his light was on late into the night so he could read it.

Night after night people popped by to see him. "Asa are you going to have a party tonight. We want to have a drink and to dance." But Asa was not interested.

Bit by bit they stopped asking him. They got the message— Asa had changed. He no longer wanted to party. Some kept away. Others started to become interested in God.

CHAPTER 4

FILLED WITH THE SPIRIT

A. A. Allen preaching

THEY TALK IN TONGUES!

When the prayer group in Hunter's house heard that Asa was saved they could not stop thanking God. God had answered their prayer. He had done the impossible. Asa was now saved. The people who used to go to the dances were now coming to meet God. When Asa turned up at one of the prayer meetings they celebrated even more.

"Lord, you've saved him. Now fill him with your Holy Spirit." The next day Asa's pastor called.

"I hear you've been up to Hunter's house. You better stay away from there! Those people are from the devil."

"What do you mean?" Asa asked. The people had seemed so friendly.

"They talk in tongues."

"What's that?"

"It sounds like a load of gibberish. You won't have to go many times before you hear it. I tell you it's of the devil. Keep away!"

Now Asa really wanted to go again. He wanted to hear them speak in tongues. He did not think they would speak nonsense, they seemed so nice. At the next meeting Asa was scared. What if his pastor was right? He was not ready to hear this language. Quietly he prayed, "Lord, please don't let these nice people talk in tongues."

That night nobody spoke in tongues. Asa kept going back. The more he went the more he wanted to hear this strange tongues thing. After several weeks he was ready to hear it. One night he did. That night everyone was worshipping God and praying to him. Then the room went quiet. One lady carried on worshipping. Her hands were lifted up to God as she praised him from her heart.

She opened her mouth and started to speak. But the words that came out were not English. She was speaking a different language. As she spoke it felt like the whole building was filled with peace. From over the other side of the room a man stood up. He started to speak in English. The words were so beautiful. Each word encouraged those there to keep following God.

"That, my friends was a message from God," the leader said. "It was given in tongues and interpreted for us here."

This was what Asa had been waiting for. His pastor had said it was from the devil, but it was so obvious that it was from God. The message encouraged people to follow God; God's peace was in that place.

WHAT ABOUT THIS VERSE PASTOR?

Asa had read all about tongues in the Bible. He knew that God gave it to help get his church strong. Now he had heard it spoken, he could not understand why his pastor was against it.

"Pastor, I've heard it!" Asa bounced up to his pastor the next day. "I've heard them speaking in tongues. It was wonderful! Now I want to be baptized in the Holy Spirit."

"You are already baptized. When I baptized you in the river you were baptized in the Holy Spirit."

"I didn't know that. But how come in Acts 2:4 when the disciples were baptized they spoke in tongues."

"Ah, that was the first Pentecost. That was special. It was only for the 12 apostles. It did not happen again."

Asa whipped his Bible out of his pocket. "But look it says that there were around 120 people there, not just the 12 apostles."

"Oh. I'd not seen that before. Umm, but it's still just a one off."

"What about Acts 10:44-46, pastor? Don't run off," Asa called, as the pastor tried to slip away. "What about Acts 19:6. When Paul laid his hands on people they received the Holy Spirit and started to speak in tongues."

"You can't have it!" the pastor screamed. "Nobody gets that kind of experience today."

"Well I am going to have it," Allen replied. "And, Pastor, you need it too!"

His pastor couldn't cope. He stormed off shouting, cursing Asa and everyone who had taught him about tongues.

CAMPING OUT FOR GOD

A few days later Asa was off camping. He went with his sister and other people from Hunter's church. They weren't going on holiday. They were going to join a Pentecostal camp. They were going to meet with God.

At the meetings Pentecostal ministers taught from the Bible. Each night they gave people an opportunity to be filled with the Holy Spirit.

Each night Asa would walk to the front to be prayed for. He was very careful when he got to the front. You see the camp did not have carpet or nice flooring. The floor was covered in sawdust. If Asa had knelt in the wrong place his clothes would have been ruined.

Every night Asa checked the floor to find the cleanest spot. Then he carefully knelt down.

Night after night he got up no different.

But even though Asa was careful, his clothes still got dirty! With two nights left to go Asa was down to his last set of clothes—a white shirt and a pair of white pants. With only two nights to go Asa was desperate to be baptized in the Holy Spirit.

"God, fill me with your Spirit!" he cried. Sweat poured down his face on to his back. His clothes were soaked in sweat. But Asa did not care anymore. He wanted God to fill him.

"Lord, I dedicate every fiber of my being, every moment of my life to you!" As he prayed, he found himself on the floor rolling around in the dirty sawdust. His suit was getting dirty, but this time he didn't care. He had to meet with God.

Then suddenly it happened. God's presence came all around him. Firstly, his fingers started to tingle. The tingling feeling crept down his wrists along his arms. Then it started in his feet. The feeling crawled up above his knees. The tingling from his feet crept towards the tingling in his hands. Asa knew that when they met in the middle something special was going to happen.

And it did. At that moment Asa was only aware of God. He knew he was in God's presence. As he lay there, he could hear a sound. Someone was shouting louder than he had ever heard. The shout was in a completely different language—one that Asa had never heard before.

As Asa drifted along in God's presence he realized who was shouting. It was him! He was speaking in tongues. He had been filled with the Holy Spirit! It was past midnight.

Most of the camp had gone to bed. But when they heard him shouting people came from across the grounds to celebrate with him.

Asa's clothes were totally ruined, but he had got what he came for. God had met him. God had filled him with the Holy Spirit. Now he was ready to go back home and serve God. But God had other plans.

CHAPTER 5

ON THE SAME PAGE

Evangelist A. A. Allen

ALL SUPPORT REMOVED

Back at home Asa felt like he was in the right place. He had Hunter and the other believers to help him. Now he also had the Holy Spirit. Finally he felt like he belonged somewhere.

But he did not have a job. There was a bad drought in the land. There had been no rain for months. The animals were dying and the plants were drying up. People were struggling to survive. Nobody could pay him to work. Asa loved it there, but he also needed to eat.

"God what do you want me to do?" he asked.

God answered by letter. Asa opened the letter and found it was from an old friend in Colorado: "Come and help me, Asa. I'm getting ready to build a barn and I need help. I'll pay you and give you somewhere to stay." Asa had no other choice. He had to go.

When Asa arrived on the ranch in September 1934 he was tired and he was thirsty. He had walked over 12 miles to reach the ranch and he could go no further. His new boss was kind, but he did not know Jesus. Asa had left all his Christian friends and had come to a place where nobody knew Jesus. He knew God wanted him there, but he felt very alone.

"Lord, please help me to win my friend to you. Please send me one other soul in this lonely place who loves you like I do."

As he looked out across the plain he could hardly see a single house. The land looked the same for miles around. Down on the ground he saw some white paper flickering.

He bent down and picked up the paper. It was a sheet of paper torn from a newsletter: The Foursquare Bridal Call. It was a newsletter from Aimee Semple McPherson—one of the most famous preachers of the time. If that newsletter was here then somebody must go to a foursquare church. That means someone here believes in Jesus!

Asa was relieved. He was not alone after all. God knew what he was doing. Now all he had to do was find out who it was. "Do you know who goes to a four-square church?" he asked his friend.

"The only one I know is that Scriven girl who lives up the road. She's religious just like you are. She goes to that church whenever she can get to town. She even thinks she's called to preach."

Asa felt so happy. He could not wait to meet her, and he did not have to wait long.

GETTING TO KNOW HER

Asa and his friends went shopping in the town. When they got home they realized they had forgotten to buy kerosene. They needed to get some before it went dark as they did not have any electricity. The kerosene fueled the lights. No fuel meant an evening of darkness.

"I think I saw the Scriven home had loads of kerosene. We could borrow some from them after supper."

His host smiled. "You know there are people who live closer than the Scrivens, but if you want to go there, we can go there." They didn't stay long and Asa did not say a word.

As they went he left his hat behind. The next night he had to go back to get it. This time he took his Bible along too. Asa wanted to spend time with Lexie Scriven. He wasn't looking for a wife, or even a girlfriend. He just wanted someone who could answer his questions about God.

For hours he asked question after question. Lexie tried to answer his questions from the Bible, but each time he would reply with another question. Lexie had been in church for a while. She had heard a lot of teaching, but she couldn't answer his questions.

Asa was digging deep. He didn't care what other people had taught her. He wanted to know what it said in the Bible. Day by day they met up to talk about what they were learning from the Bible. Day after day they both grew closer to Jesus.

Lexie didn't know it, but she was falling in love with Asa, the man who was inspiring her to follow Jesus more closely. Then she had some bad news.

"I'm going home in a few days' time." Asa had come to see her. "My mom needs help selling the farm and moving. I won't be coming back."

Lexie was in shock. She wanted to make him stay, but she didn't want to stop him from doing what he wanted. Lexie took a deep breath. Quietly she prayed to God, "Thank you God that he has been in my life for this short time. Bless him as he moves on from here."

As the days went by Lexie missed Asa. She carried on studying the Bible and looking for answers to her questions there. Now she did it alone.

But it was not the end of their friendship. Asa started to write every day. The letters were friendly. They told her how people were being saved. They spoke about the people he was meeting. They talked about the church he was going to and they told her what he was learning about.

THE GIFTS OF THE SPIRIT

"Desire the best gifts."

Asa had been reading 1 Corinthians 14. There was a long list of gifts that the Holy Spirit gives there and God then said we should want the best gifts. "God give me the best ones. I really want the best gift that you have for me."

As he sat in church that Sunday "I'd love to interpret tongues." Asa thought to himself.

At that moment a lady stood up and spoke in tongues. Somehow Asa just knew the first line of what she was saying. Then he understood the second line. But he couldn't hear anymore.

"God, if you tell me what the rest of it means, I'll stand up and tell everyone else."

But God didn't tell him. Instead God replied, "If you tell the people what I've told you so far, I'll tell you what the rest of it means."

Asa felt embarrassed. What if he started and couldn't finish it? People would think he was silly. Surely he needed to know more than the first line? As he sat there waiting to hear more, a lady at the back stood up.

"God has told me what the message in tongues means," she started. The words she spoke where the same words Asa had heard, but somehow she got the whole message. Asa wanted to know how she did it. At the end of the meeting Asa ran over to her. "When you understand tongues, do you get it all at once, or a bit at a time?"

"I only get a bit at a time," she replied. "I've found that when I have shared the bit I know God gives me the next bit."

"What would you do if you shared the first bit and God doesn't give you anymore. Aren't you scared you'll just be stood there looking silly?"

"If you're afraid of that you may as well not start. God gives us gifts to use them. The whole point of them is to help other people. We have to trust God, that's what faith is. You can't be afraid of what other people think. Fear is the opposite of faith."

READY FOR MARRIAGE

Lexie continued learning. She wanted to go to Bible school and Asa was excited for her. "I'd love to join you," he said. But he did not know how it would happen. Asa kept on writing letters. But one letter was different from any he had sent before.

Dear Lexie,

I guess you've worked out by now that I love you. I didn't realize how much I loved you until you decided to go to school. Then I started to think, 'she'll find a nice young man who she can love. It won't be long before she has forgotten all about me.'

I can't let that happen without telling you first how I feel. Could it possibly be true that you love me too?

For the first time Asa and Lexie admitted that they were more than just friends. They wanted to be married. Asa travelled back to Lexie. A few days later, on Wednesday, September 19, 1936 they were married. They did not have much money, but they did love each other and God.

They also had a plan.

CHAPTER 6

IN TRAINING

People in prayer during a meeting

OFF TO BIBLE SCHOOL

Asa and Lexie had it all worked out.

A few days after they were married the happy couple set off to start Bible School. Between them they had saved up enough money to pay for the college and live for the year. Their little car was packed full of everything they owned in the world as they set off on the adventure.

This year would be just what they needed to get ready for the ministry.

On the way they stopped over to see Asa's mom.

When they saw her they were shocked. She was very sick. Worse still she did not even have any decent food in the house.

They knew they had to help her. Using some of their college money and went out and bought food to give her strength. For the next few days they looked after Asa's mother as she got better.

By the time she was well, they had used nearly all of their money to help her. Now there was no way they could afford to live and pay for both of them to go to school. Perhaps one of them could go and the other could work to earn money. They did not know what they were going to do, but they were sure God had a plan.

When they turned up at the college they had to find somewhere to live. "We'll work for you on your farm if you can give us somewhere to live and food to eat," they offered. But no one could help them.

They had no food, no money and no real options. There was only one thing for it, they would have to go back home.

"I'm sure we were doing what God wanted us to do. How could it have gone so wrong?" they asked each other. Back at home they could still not find any work to do.

HOW MUCH WOOD CAN YOU CHOP?

"You could always chop down the trees in the wood out back," his mom suggested. "If you've got an axe and saw you can get a dollar for a huge pile."

"But we don't have an axe or a saw. I don't think we've got enough money to buy them either." Asa protested.

"You could borrow somebody else's tools. They'll pay you 75 cents," she replied.

That night they went to a neighbor to borrow his axe. The next morning they set out early, ready to get chopping.

All day they worked hard, cutting a tree into logs. By evening they had finished their first pile. They had earned their first 75 cents. After a few weeks work they could afford their own tools. Now they were earning a dollar each day.

At last things were getting easier, but their dream of going to Bible school had been shattered. They had to wait until God showed them what was next.

THE FIRST MEETING

"You know Asa and Lexie are called to the ministry."

Asa and Lexie had popped round to see a neighbor. She was chatting to a friend who had come to visit. The friend looked up. "People really need God where I live. There's no church. Why don't you come over? My living room is quite big, we can meet there. If you come, I'll invite the neighbors."

Asa had not been to Bible school. He had not been ordained a minister. But God was giving him somewhere to preach so Asa went. Each night Asa preached. The first night the room was full and three people came forward at the end crying. They wanted to give their life to Jesus. All three of them left with huge smiles on their faces. They knew God had taken their sin away.

The next night even more people came. After a few nights people were walking for six miles, just to get to the meeting. People filled the living room and the kitchen. Each day Asa and Lexie went to the wood to work. Each evening they went to the house to preach.

After two weeks Asa had no sermons left to preach. He was tired and they were running out of food. But God knew what they needed. That night they were given their first offering and could get some food.

The same night a lady invited them to go and preach in her local schoolhouse. "It's a pretty rough place," she explained. "Preachers have been there before but the people have chased them out of town. There will probably be trouble, but you're welcome to try!"

Asa was used to rough people. He had been one himself. He was ready to go anywhere that would let him preach.

CHAPTER 7

A NEW LIFE

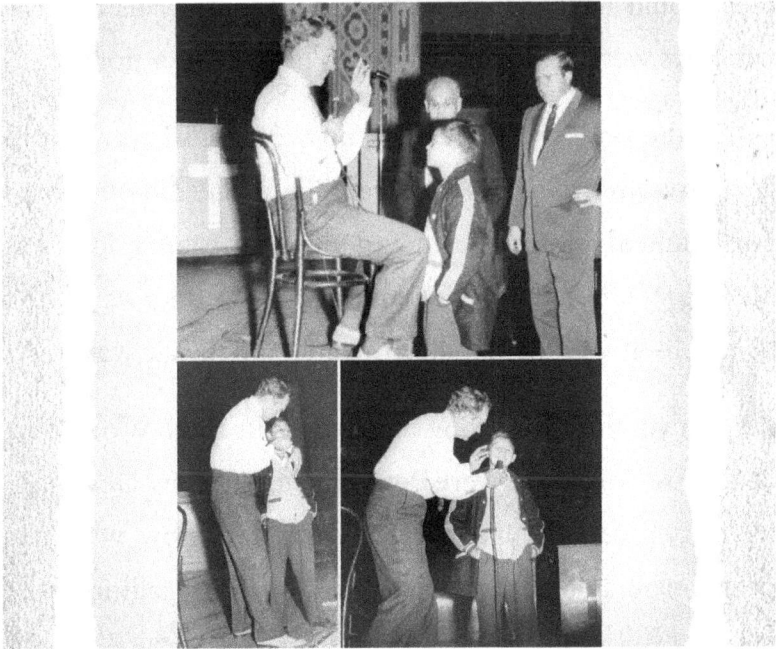

A. A. Allen prays for a boy

HOME SWEET HOME

The schoolhouse was too far from home for them to travel each day. Asa and Lexie had to move there. When they arrived they found that they could use the school house, but there was nowhere to live.

All day they searched through the town. As evening came they had only found one free place: a small cabin.

"Well, Lexie, at least we will have a roof over our heads," Asa said.

When they got inside they realized that was about all they would have. There were cracks in the walls and the windows were broken. This was to be their new home.

By the time they had hung up a couple of blankets to cover over the gaps it almost felt like home. No one could pop round and knock on their door as the cabin's door was missing. Even the quilt they hung over the doorway didn't do much—it was the middle of winter and the air was cold!

Can you imagine living in a house like that? Would you do it? Asa and Lexie were determined to follow God's call, no matter what happened. They did not know what the people would do to them and their house was falling apart, but they still went.

People came to the meetings. They didn't try to throw them out of town, but they didn't get saved either. As Asa spoke people were convicted, but still nobody responded to the Gospel.

After two weeks of preaching nobody had come forward to accept Jesus. Not even one.

Asa knew there was only one way they were going to see people saved—they would have to pray and pray, and then pray some more.

PRAYING THROUGH THE NIGHT

"Lexie, let's stay up all night and pray for the lost in this place."

They didn't have much fuel for their lamp so they turned it off and huddled round the fire. The fire gave them a little bit of light so they could see each other. More importantly it kept them warm.

For the first hour they prayed passionately for the lost. One by one they prayed for the people who had been coming to the meetings. When they had prayed for everything that they could think of Lexie started to nod off.

"Wake up!" Asa prodded her. "We promised God we would stay up all night to pray for them. We must keep our promise!" Lexie woke with a start. A few minutes later Asa started to breathe heavily. Now he was drifting off to sleep. Lexie poked Asa and he stirred.

For the rest of the night they prayed and poked each other so that they would stay awake. When morning came they fell into bed and slept for a few hours. That night they could not wait to see how God would answer their prayers.

ONE BY ONE

The meeting started as usual. The same number of people came. The people sang the song as they had done on previous nights. The preaching was the same as on other nights.

Everything was the same until Asa invited people to give their lives to Jesus.

When the altar call was given a young teenager came forward! He was the only one who came, but God was working in him. He knelt at the front weeping. He knew he was sinner and he stayed kneeling for over five minutes until he had found Jesus.

The rest of the congregation sat and watched him, nobody moved forward and nobody left the building.

When he got up he was smiling. He walked over to an older man. "Dad, you've got to give your heart to Jesus. He is the only one who can forgive sins. Please go forward, I beg you."

The man got up and went to the front. A few minutes later the man and his son both stood grinning. They had found Jesus. Together the two went to a group of teenage girls. There the boy found his sister. As they got near to her she started to cry. She jumped up and ran to the front.

Everyone else kept watching.

On and on it went. One at a time people came forward to find Jesus. Asa simply sat back and watched—God was doing all the work.

For two and a half hours the whole congregation sat there. Nobody got up except to go to the front. There was never more than one person at the front, but by the end of the time 23 people had become Christians. Not only that, but the people had forgiven each other for things they had done wrong.

At midnight Asa, Lexie and the 23 new believers all knelt and started to pray for those in the town who did not know Jesus. Other Christians now came forward who were willing to help. God had answered their prayers.

IT'S GOOD TO SERVE GOD

Back in bed that night they were so excited they could hardly sleep. The next morning they got up early and leapt out of bed. As soon as they got up they wished they hadn't. There was no food in the house. The last of their beans had been eaten the night before.

As they stood there wondering what to do, someone came to the house. A man stood in the doorway. He was holding a cardboard box. Asa had not met him before. "My two children were saved last night thanks to you. I've not been there myself but I'm right glad with what you are doing."

"I thought you might be able to use some groceries," he added as he gave them the box. "Let me know if there is anything else I can do."

When they opened the box there was ham, fresh eggs and milk, homemade bread, butter and honey. For a couple who had been living off beans and corn it was a feast—the best meal they had had in weeks.

All thoughts of going to Bible school were now in the past. Asa A. Allen was now doing what God had called him to do. When he had finished his work there he knew that God would move him on - and God did.

CHAPTER 8

MOVING ON

A. A. Allen praying for a lady

THEIR 2ND HOME

When God told them to move to a new town they had to find a new home. The new town only had one empty property. Like their last home it was full of cracks and gaps. Outside it was winter. Ice covered the ground as the cold air blew through the house.

As the ice melted their house started to leak. Not just one small leak, but dozens of them. They could not put their bed anywhere in the house without it getting wet. The best they could do was make sure no water fell on their heads while they slept. They covered the rest of the bed so that the water would run off on to the floor.

When they got out of bed in the morning they had to wade through water. Now that's gross! "Lexie," Asa said one day, "we need to ask God for money." Anyone looking at them would agree. They had no real home and no proper food.

"It says in the book of James in the Bible that we don't have things because we don't ask. Let's ask God to give us $200." That same day someone gave them 35 cents.

"It's a start," Lexie said. She wrote the date and the amount in a notebook. "Whenever we get money that is obviously from God, I'm going to write it in here, until we have the $200 that we asked God for."

AN EMPTY BUILDING

When God sent them on to another town, Asa found an empty building. It had been used for a church to meet. Nobody had been in there for years except for some birds that had made it their home. Asa had walked the whole way there. He couldn't drive because he had no money to put gas in his tank.

The next day someone sent them $5. Now he could fill the car up and they could eat. Once again God had provided just in time.

On the first night it was raining hard. Most people stayed indoors. Only one man turned up. The man gave his life to Jesus. The meeting was worth it. The next day they popped round to see the new Christian. When Asa walked into their home he knew the family was poor.

Their home had one small room and two beds. The man lived, ate and slept in that room with his wife and six children. The children were skinny and their clothes were all worn. Asa and Lexie spent some time with the happy family, praying with them and sharing more of Jesus.

When it was time for them to go the man got up. "Here, take these," he said, and he thrust a bag into Asa's hand. Asa opened the bag. There were two brown eggs inside. "You can have one each for breakfast," the man smiled.

Asa looked at the family. They needed these eggs more than he did. "Please, give them to your children," Asa begged. "Brother Allen, Jesus saved me last night. I want to do something for him. I love him so much. I feel he wants me to do this for you. Please don't stop me from doing what God's asked me to do, will you?"

Asa could not reply. He knew he had to take them. Tears ran down his cheeks as he accepted the eggs. More tears came as they ate the eggs the next morning. They could not stop thanking God.

AN EGGY REWARD

That night the rain had stopped and the church was half full. As the first song began the egg man came running in. He was holding a small brown paper bag.

"Look! Look! Can you see? There are four eggs in here. Every single one of my hens laid an egg today. They have hardly laid a single egg for three months, now they have laid four!"

He gave them to Asa. "I want you to have them." The next night the egg man came just as the meetings had started. This time in his brown bag he had eight eggs.

"Brother Allen, they are all for you!" he said passing them over. God was doing a little miracle and getting those hens laying eggs. The man, and everyone else, was finding out that you can't give more than God can give back to you.

The next night the man looked like he was going to pop with excitement. When it was time to share testimonies he was the first to stand up.

"First I gave the preacher two eggs. The next day my hens laid four eggs. I gave them all to the preacher and the next day the hens laid eight eggs. I gave all of these to the preacher and today they laid twelve eggs!"

His hens had laid enough eggs for him to sell. God was looking after his family.

BIBLE SCHOOL?

Asa had wanted to go to Bible School, but God had other plans for him. God wanted to teach him direct from the Bible. Asa tried to get a job to earn money, but there was no work available. He had no choice! Instead he spent the days praying and studying the Bible.

In the meetings he let people ask any question that they wanted to. Then he and Lexie would go home and study the Bible to find the answer to people's questions. They wanted every answer they gave to be from the Bible. God was teaching them and then they were living it straight away.

He was also showing them how it applied to real people in real situations. For some people God sends them to Bible

School for others God brings the Bible School to them. God had created a course just for them to learn what he wanted to teach them.

But there was one area that Asa did not understand. "So many people are suffering. So many people are sick. God promises that if I lay hands on sick people they will get better. Some of them do, but most of them walk away just as sick as when they came. I know there is nothing wrong with God, so there must be something wrong with me."

For hours at a time Asa would seek God. "God please show me what's wrong with me. Show me what is stopping you from using me to do miracles." He kept on asking God.

God was getting him ready to hear the answer.

CHAPTER 9

SO YOU WANT GOD TO USE YOU?

Crowds responding to an altar call

I *MUST* HEAR FROM GOD

Asa was desperate. By now he had become the pastor of a church. God was doing things, but he still wasn't seeing lots of healings. "I am not going to eat. I am going to fast and pray until God speaks to me," Asa told his wife. It wasn't that easy. Every time he tried to fast he found he was in the middle of a battle.

He would start praying for a few hours. Then he would smell the food wafting under the door. Before he knew it Asa was sat at the table eating with them. He had stopped fasting before God had answered. The next day Asa went to pray again. This time he found that he felt really tired. "I think I will go and rest now, then I can carry on praying tomorrow," he told himself.

And so it went on. Day after day he started to pray, but he kept stopping to eat. Lexie always kept a place for him at the table. She knew that he would join them soon enough. Asa had come out of his prayer room yet again to eat with his family. As he put food to his mouth he heard God speak to him.

"Asa, until you want to hear from me more than anything else in the world I will not answer you."

Asa looked at the food. Did he want God to use him more than he wanted to eat? Did he really want to find out why he was not seeing miracles regularly? He got up from the table. "Honey, I am going to pray. This time I do mean business. Lock me in to the closet and leave me there. I am going to keep on praying until I hear from God."

"You'll be asking me to open the door for you in around an hour. I know you." As she locked the door behind him she called, "I'll let you out as soon as you knock."

"I will not knock until I get the answer that I have been waiting for!" Asa replied. This time he really was serious.

GOD TURNS UP

Hour after hour Asa prayed. Many times he felt so close to giving up, but he carried on. At times he thought about how he didn't really need to see God move in this way. He could just carry on serving God like he had been.

Each time he was about to stop he would remember that he really wanted to see God move like in the Bible. He would carry on praying until God answered or until he died. He would not quit.

After many hours the closet began to change. Light started to fill it. Asa turned round to look at the door. He thought his wife must have opened it. It was still locked shut. This light was coming from heaven. God had opened up the door of heaven and God's glory was pouring in. God came closer and closer. God's presence was so powerful Asa thought he might die.

Still he asked the same question, "Lord, why can't I heal the sick? Why can't I work miracles in your name? Why do I not see signs following like Peter, John and Paul did in the Bible?"

At that moment he heard a whirlwind stirring around him. As Asa listened, he realized God was speaking quickly and clearly. Asa hadn't expected such a clear answer. He did not realize that God had such a long list of things for him to deal with. He knew he had to write down everything God was saying. If only he had brought pen and paper into the closet with him.

He looked around and found a broken pencil. He sharpened it with his teeth. Then he pulled out a cardboard box filled with clothes and started to write on the side of it.

"Lord, please can you start again so that I can write down all you say to me."

God started the list again.

GOD HAS SPOKEN

This is what God told Asa he had to do:

1. The disciple is not above his master (Luke 6:40): You must not expect to do greater things than Jesus or to be

greater than him. Jesus was persecuted, so you should expect persecution too.

2. Everyone that is perfect will be like his master (Luke 6:40): You can do the same things that Jesus did. It is possible. We can be like Jesus, not only in the power he shows but in the way he lived his life.

3. Be perfect, even as your father in heaven is perfect (Matthew 5:48): God wants us to be perfect and he helps us to live as he wants us to live. It's a high standard, but one that we have to aim for.

4. Christ is our example: To live as Jesus lived, we need to think as he thinks. Jesus lived his life led by the Holy Spirit. We need to do the same.

5. If anyone wants to follow me they need to deny themselves … (Luke 9:23): If anyone wants to follow Jesus they have to turn away from what they want, to follow what God wants. Pray even when you don't feel like it. Spend time with Jesus instead of just playing around. It's hard to do it sometimes, there are hundreds of great things you could be doing and want to be doing, but that's what it means to really follow Jesus—we don't do what we want to do, we do what HE wants us to do.

6. … take up their cross every day and follow me. (Luke 9:23). Every day has to be set aside for God. You never get a holiday when you are serving Jesus. Every day of our lives should be given to him if we really want him to use us.

7. I must decrease, (John 3:30). When God uses us it is not so that we look great. In fact the more he uses us the less people should notice us. Instead they should see Jesus.

8. He must increase, (John 3:30). As we become less, Jesus should be seen more clearly. When we understand that we need God for everything then he can shine through us. After all we can't do anything without him. We need more and more of Jesus every day if he is to be able to use us more and more.

9. Be careful what words you speak, don't say foolish things. The words that come out of our mouth show us what's really going on in our heart. We need to watch every word we say and not just talk for the sake of talking. Think before you speak!

10. Present your body. When we give our bodies to Jesus he can use us as he chooses. That means he decides what we do every day of the week (not just on Sundays).

11. Part of his divine nature. We need to be plugged into God so that he can work through us. As we believe what God said we get to be part of his plan for the world. Simply believing God brings about change.

12. Asa never told anybody what the final two items on the list were. He didn't even tell his wife! They were two sins that he struggled with.

Every person fights against a particular sin in their life. Maybe we make excuses for why it is okay to do these things. But Asa found that it is only when we admit that these things are wrong and deal with these sins that God can really use us.

"Asa," God said, "this is your answer. When you have done all of these things on the list then you will not only heal the sick, but in my name you will cast out demons. You will see mighty miracles as you preach the word for I will give you power over all the power of the enemy.

The light started to leave the closet. Asa banged on the door and waited for his wife to let him out. God had spoken to him. Now he knew what to do. The next challenge was doing it. Asa started to work his way through the list one at a time, ticking off each thing as he conquered it.

GOD IS CALLING ME

A woman shares what God has done for her

GO TO IDAHO

Asa and Lexie both heard God telling them to go to a small town in Idaho. "New Meadows" was a small town with 300 people in it. When they got there no one wanted to give them a building. They were a bit confused until a friend suggested they go to a town a few miles down the road.

They arrived with only 40 cents. They had kept this money to buy food for their new baby.

It was Saturday.

"I'm going to preach on Sunday," Asa told his wife.

They had no money to hire a hall, they did not know anybody, but they knew that God had called them to be there.

"You can't have my hall unless you pay me $10 for the month," the owner told Asa.

"I will pay you on Monday," Asa promised.

"You preachers are all the same you promise to pay but then you don't. But I'll tell you what we'll do. You can have the hall for $10 a month but you must pay me on Monday. No money and you will have to leave."

Asa was excited. God had given them a hall. They could preach there and live there. Lexie put a curtain up at the back of the room. This would be their home. The rest of the space would be for the meetings.

Asa walked around the town that afternoon telling people what he was doing. One man smiled, "we've been praying for two years for God to send someone. We'll be there on Sunday."

GOD LOVES TO GIVE

The first lady who walked into the building shook his hand, "thank you so much for coming here. God bless you." As she walked off Asa discovered she had left $10 in his hand. God had given him the rent that he needed.

By the time the service started there were 59 people ready to worship God. During the service Asa took up an offering which gave him enough money to feed his family for the whole week. God had been getting everything ready for Asa. Now God was helping him to stay there.

Asa couldn't help but smile at each person as they left. God still had one more surprise for Asa. "God told me to give you $12," one lady said on her way out. She did not know that was the exact amount that Asa needed to pay for his car.

Of course God could have given them a big offering to pay for food, the rent and the car. By sending three people with three different amounts to cover the three different bills God was showing them that he was in charge. God really wanted them there. They needed to know this, because not everything in their life was going to be easy.

MOVE ON

Asa was busy chopping wood. The church had not grown. In fact, there was only one family left in the church. God spoke to Asa, "*Now* it is time for you to go to New Meadows."

Asa put down his axe and ran to Lexie. "God says it's time to go darling so let's pack."

The one church member decided to join them. In the first meeting five people were saved. Every single service someone else was saved. God was doing a great work. Not only that, he was giving them what they needed. The manager of the local food store had been holding meetings in his home. He wanted to bless Asa so he gave them their food for free! They were blessed.

Before long the room they were meeting in was too small. So they moved to a larger cabin. And more people kept coming. "So many of us are following God now! We need to start a church."

When the manager of the store heard about it he was furious. "I am the only leader around here. I am the one in charge. I've been running meetings much longer than Asa Allen has."

The revival had started in a building owned by the manager. They were living in a home that belonged to the manager. So they had to listen to him when he came to them one night. "God says your time here is over. You have to move on." He told them bluntly.

Asa was not so sure. They were happy to move if God told them to, but they didn't think it was God speaking. Asa and Lexie asked God what they should do. God showed them very clearly that the manager was not a pastor or a leader in the church. He never had been and he never would be. God wanted them to stay.

They would have no food and nowhere to live, but if God wanted them to stay they would.

Asa spoke to each of the new Christians and told them what was happening. If you want us to stay we will stay, if you want us to go we will go. The Christians voted that night. Every single one of them felt God wanted them to stay except the manager.

Asa and Lexie moved out of their home into a new one. They lived off the small amount that the people could afford to give. They were poor, but happy, and people were being saved.

The church grew so much that they had to build a new building. God was using them in New Meadows, just as he promised he would.

CHAPTER 11

SOMEBODY'S GOT TO HELP HIM

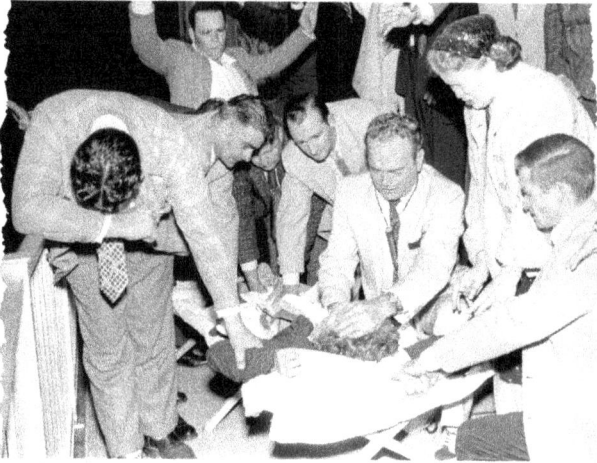

A.A. ALLEN
THE MIRACLE MAN

A sick lady is prayed for

GETTING COLD FEET

It was Sunday morning. And it was cold. Outside a white blanket of snow covered the ground. Asa got up early to light a fire in the church. He wanted the building to be warm when the people arrived. He left the fire burning and went back home.

Fifteen minutes before the service began Asa came back to the church. Next to the fire stood a boy in rags. His clothes were torn, his shoes had huge holes in them and his feet were frozen. He had walked the whole way.

Immediately Asa recognized the boy. His dad was a drunk. Even standing next to the fire, the boy was still cold. He took the child home and Lexie warmed him up. When he came back he was wearing a pair of warm socks. His shoes were back in the house drying out.

During the service Asa couldn't take his eyes off the boy's feet. The poor boy would have to walk home through the snow again. His shoes were falling apart. Asa remembered the kind man who had given him his first pair of shoes when he was a child. Surely somebody would help this boy.

Two people in the congregation were rich enough to help. Neither of them did. One lady drove off in her car before Asa had a chance to ask her if she would take the boy home. She lived near to his house and it would have been easy for her to help. But she didn't.

WE HAVE THE ANSWER

Lexie brought out the boy's shoes. She bent down to put them back on his feet. As she did so she glanced over at her own son's feet. They were the same size! She compared the shoes. They were warm and cozy. "Jimmie take your shoes off," she said.

Asa looked on. They had just had a baby and could not even afford clothes for the baby. How would they give away Jimmie's clothes? But he knew that he could not let the boy walk in the snow as he was.

"What will I do for shoes, Mama?" their son asked.

"You don't need them as badly as he does. Besides Jesus said 'Give and it will be given to you,' so Jesus will give you another pair."

Jimmie took his shoes off and gave them to the boy. Asa couldn't watch any more. He had to go and pray. "God, why didn't you get someone else to give them? You know we can't afford it." By the time he had finished praying he knew that they had done what God wanted them to do.

GOD SENDS THEM MONEY

The next morning a letter came in the mail. Inside was $20. "Mama, will there be enough there to buy me new shoes."

"There sure will," she smiled. Then she paused. Asa knew what she was doing. She was listening to God. He also knew what God was saying because God had just spoken to him too.

"Let's give half of it to our friend the evangelist," he said.

"Let's give ALL of it to him," she replied.

They both knew that God had spoken. They both knew that their friend really needed the money.

Asa rushed to the evangelist. "Here is $10," he said.

"I can't take that from you Ace," the man said. "I know how much you need the money yourself."

Asa was relieved. But then he knew he had done something wrong. God had told them to give it ALL to this man. He had only offered half.

"Please!" he cried out, "Please take it all. God told me to give you all $20. I have to do it."

The man smiled and started to praise God. It was just what he needed. If God wanted them to give it, then he knew God wanted him to take it. All that day Asa wondered how they would survive. All day they had peace because they knew that they had obeyed God.

The next morning another letter arrived in the post. Inside was a check for $50. Asa had never seen so much money. The note said, "I couldn't sleep tonight. God told me you would need this money in the morning. I planned to wait until then but God told me to get up and send it straight away."

They had given away a pair of shoes and $20 to people who really needed it. Now God had sent them $50. God had an even greater to gift to give them. The next Sunday a man staggered forward. He was the father of the boy with cold feet. As he came forward his friend joined him and several members of their family. All of them knelt and gave their lives to Jesus.

"Brother Allen, I hate preachers," the man said. "I always have. I've said all kind of bad things about you. But when my son came home last week I saw God's love for the first time. You took the shoes off your own son's feet and gave them to my son. I could stand it no longer. I had to come."

That Sunday Jimmie and the drunkard's son sat side by side. Jimmie held his feet out.

"Look at my new shoes," Jimmie said. "Mama said Jesus would give me new ones if I gave you mine and Jesus did it!"

Because of that one action many people were saved. That one act of love was bigger than any miracle of healing. That one action showed God to people who would never have come near a church. That one action also built up young Jimmie's faith as he learned that it is better to give things away than to receive.

CHAPTER 12

THE LIST IS NOT COMPLETE

A. A. Allen praying for the sick

LIFE CARRIES ON

Asa carried on serving God. Every four and a half years God moved him and his family on to start a new church.

Asa began travelling around the country to preach the Gospel. Life did not get much easier. Often they did not have much money. Asa travelled by himself and was away from his family for long periods at a time.

Back at home his children sometimes didn't even recognize him.

Other evangelists were stopping to get regular jobs. There was a war on and nobody could afford to look after them properly. But Asa kept going.

As he preached his voice felt tighter and tighter. Soon it was nearly impossible for him to preach. He definitely could not sing. He was only young and he had not done everything that God called him to do. He started to worry.

"I don't know how much longer I can do this for. If I can't speak I certainly can't preach." Every sermon he preached could have been his last one.

Finally he went to see a doctor. The doctor looked in his throat, "Preacher, your preaching days are over!" the doctor announced. "Your vocal chords are totally ruined. Find a job where you do not need to talk otherwise soon you won't be able to talk at all. Go and live in Arizona or somewhere dry and work for the defense department."

That was just what Asa feared. His preaching days were over. But Asa was not going to give up that easily. He went to see a second doctor. The doctor looked in his throat. "Preacher, your preaching days are over!" the doctor announced. "Your vocal chords are totally ruined. Find a job where you do not need to talk otherwise soon you won't be able to talk at all. Go and live in Arizona or somewhere dry and work for the defense department."

Asa went to see a third doctor. "Preacher, …"

Asa interrupted him. "I know what you are going to say. But I am not going to stop preaching and I am not moving to Arizona. Nor am I going to work for the defense department. I will preach until I cannot talk and then I will write my sermons up on a board for people to read."

The doctor was amazed. How did Asa know what he was about to say? Asa didn't know who would want to listen to him. How could he preach about the sick being healed if he couldn't even talk himself! But he was not going to stop doing what God had called him to do.

As he walked home he was scared. The same fear he had felt as a child now started to take over his life again. What would happen in the future? The fear was so strong that he could hardly breathe.

At that moment a Bible verse popped into his head: 2 Timothy 1:7, "God has not given you a spirit of fear." So fear was a spirit.

He went to see a pastor. "Please pray for me and cast out the spirit of fear."

As the pastor prayed Asa was set free from fear. He started to praise God. As he praised, he found he could shout louder than he had shouted for months. God had healed him.

TORMENTED

Asa had been the pastor of a church for a while now. The church had doubled in size and they had built an extension to the building. God was really blessing them. Lexie was happy. Asa was not travelling around as much; they had a stable salary from the church and a nice home to live in. Their life was still busy as any pastor's home is, but at least their life was more normal.

Asa was not satisfied. Sure there were hundreds of people coming to the church, but there were millions of people who were not. If only he could reach all of them.

It was then that an idea popped into his head. Nearly every home had a radio. If he could speak on the radio loads more people could hear the Gospel. He raced to the church leaders and told them his plans. They felt tired just thinking about it.

"We've grown fast, pastor and that is good. Now let's take a bit of time to settle down. We don't think we should be doing any radio programs at this time."

Asa felt like he had been punched. He had so much desire to serve God and now he had been told no. Maybe they were right, but he wasn't happy. He started to sob uncontrollably. Sometimes he would cry out.

"He's having a break down," the leaders said when they saw him. "Let's pay for him to have a long holiday." They wanted their pastor to get better as soon as possible. Asa and Lexie drove to the mountains. All the way there Asa felt in pain. At night he could not sleep. When they got to a house in the middle of nowhere he could not rest.

"Let's go home and be around our people again," Asa said. And so they got in the car for the three day journey home. But it did not help! There was no way forward.

"I just feel so tormented. I wish I could sleep properly," Asa wept.

He was a grown man acting like a small child. He was a mess. Asa pulled the car over. Lexie turned to him. "Lexie, pray for me. Cast out this tormenting demon." Lexie put her hand on his shoulder and prayed, "In Jesus name I command you GO!" When she prayed he felt something disappear from his stomach.

For three whole days and three nights Asa slept and slept and slept. When he woke up he was ready to serve God again. He did not know what God had planned for him.

I MUST PROTECT MY FLOCK

"These men are making history."

Stories of a new breed of special preachers were going around the churches. Thousands were flocking to hear them preach. These men were not the best speakers ever, but when they prayed for the sick, the sick were healed! Asa read about them and laughed. There were stories of deaf people being healed and cancers falling out of bodies. Every known sickness was being healed.

"These people are a bunch of fanatics. They are religious loonies," he thought.

Asa had always preached that God could heal, but did God really heal people from cancer today? He had been told by God what he had to do if he wanted to see these miracles. In fact God had given him a whole list of things to do. But he had been so busy building a church that he had missed what God was doing in the rest of the church.

"These evangelists are probably just trying to get a crowd. It's only a publicity stunt," he thought to himself. "I must protect my people from these men."

When some of Asa's friends were going to a meeting, he decided to go along to see for himself. The evangelist was a man called Oral Roberts. As Asa walked into the tent he thought about the list God had given him. He still kept the list in the Bible and he had marked off every single item except the last two.

As Asa sat in the tent he was convicted by what he saw. Oral Roberts was doing what God had called Asa to do. Oral had obeyed God. Asa had not. He had not paid the price. He saw there watching the miracles and the crowds. His heart was stirred as he saw hundreds rush to the front in tears to give their lives to Jesus. At that moment Asa knew that this was not a fanatic. This was a man who was serving God. He was a man who wanted to see people saved.

Asa wept.

God spoke to him, "My son, eleven years ago you asked me to show you what you had to do to move in miracles. I showed you 13 things that you had to do. You have only done 11 of them. Eleven years ago I called you to the same ministry, but you have only done part of what I called you to do. I told you the price but you have not paid it. You have failed to do what I called you to do."

"I'll do it Lord, I am so sorry, I'll do it."

As soon as Asa got home he resigned his job as pastor. God had called him to preach the Gospel with signs and wonders. God had called him to be an evangelist. Asa was going to do what God had called him to do.

CHAPTER 13

THE REAL WORK BEGINS

Crowds at a service in Cuba

SIGN AND WONDERS

Asa looked out at the crowd. Last week he had left his church. This week God had opened the door for him to be an evangelist. All over the place pastors wanted him to come to them. God was moving across the nation. Now Asa was a part of that move. He was seeing more people healed than ever before. But still some people were going away disappointed.

One campaign took him to California. While he was in the middle of the campaign he took out the list to look at it again. There was only one thing left on it. He had tried but he could not beat it. He knew other pastors who struggled as he did, so he was no different from them, but he knew that God was calling him to live for him 100%. God had told him what he had to do. Surely he should be able to do it.

Asa spent time praying and finally gave the last area over to God. He took out a pen and crossed the last item off the list. He was ready.

As Asa went into the pulpit that night he knew that God was going to do something. God's presence was on the congregation like he had never seen it before. Night after night God came with his power. Many people were healed without anyone even praying for them. They sat in their seat and were instantly healed. Anyone watching could see the miracles.

Tumors fell off people. Crippled people were made whole. Goiters, swellings in the throat, disappeared. Blind people started to see. Not only that, but people came back night after night to tell what God had done. Some brought with them reports from their doctors and X-rays that proved that they had been healed.

Night after night people were healed, delivered and best of all more people than ever were getting saved. Asa had done what God had told him to do. Now God was doing what he promised he would do. Asa saw that some people needed help so that they would come ready to be healed. So he wrote a book to help people: God's guarantee to heal you. Thousands of people were healed as they read it.

ONWARD AND FORWARD

Asa was travelling more and more. Lexie longed to be with her husband, so they bought a trailer and travelled together. Their children were schooled in the trailer and travelled everywhere with their parents.

The more they travelled the bigger the crowds got. They realized that they needed a tent. They didn't tell anyone what they were thinking, instead they prayed about it.

One day a lady came to see Asa. "Brother Allen, God told me to give you this."

"What is it?" Asa asked.

"It's an offering that God told me to give you. It is to help you buy a large tent. Your ministry should not be limited to small buildings. God has shown me that you will preach to thousands at a time."

Asa was so excited; God had given him the first $600. He couldn't wait to share the news with the pastor of the church he was ministering in. That night Asa was surprised when the pastor stood up to take an offering. "God is telling Asa Allen to buy a tent, so let's give money to him to do that." Asa walked away from the meeting with another $500.

Asa never asked anyone for money, but people kept giving him money. Before long he had $1500. Now he just needed to find out how much a tent would cost.

"You'll need $6000, if you want it big enough to fit everyone in," a tent maker told him. "Don't forget you'll need to buy seats and a PA system too."

Asa knew they still had a long way to go. God had helped them so far. He was leading them. Surely, he would make a way for this to work. When Asa heard that a minister was selling a huge tent, complete with all the equipment he would need for only $8500 he knew God was in it.

But he still only had $1500.

Asa picked up the phone. "I've only got $1500, but you can have it all as the first payment for the tent."

The owner had been offered cash for the full amount from someone else, but he told Asa he would pray about it. The next morning the man called, "You can have the tent and all the equipment. Pay me $1500 now and $100 every night you use the tent until you've paid it all."

Asa was not surprised. After all if God wanted him to have it, it was his. Now all he needed was two large trucks to carry the equipment around. After he preached that night the crowd heard what he needed. One after another gave him money for the trucks. By the end of the meeting the trucks were paid for.

The A. A. Allen Revival Tent was ready for action. On July 4, 1951 in Washington DC Asa held his first tent meeting. The ministry was growing fast. Asa knew it needed a good structure to handle the money. He set up an organization and paid himself a small salary. Every other penny people gave him would go back to the ministry.

SPREADING THE GOOD NEWS

All through the summer of 1951 Asa preached and the tent was filled. He could not preach in the tent in winter, it would be too cold. If only he could take the tent to Latin America. It was warmer there and he longed to see many people saved. The only problem was that these people there were too poor to pay for the cost of the tent.

God knew what was on his heart. By the end of the summer God had given him enough money to pay for crusades through the winter. Asa and his tent set off for Havan in Cuba. That winter thousands of people came to Jesus.

The local priests were not happy, but the people were delighted to be meeting with the real Jesus. And so Asa had a pattern. In the summer months he travelled through North America. In winter he travelled to Cuba. But he still wanted to reach even more people.

Asa remembered his dream of preaching to people on the radio. It was time for that dream to become a reality. In November 1953 the Allen Revival Hour started on radio. In 1954 Asa was taking his tent around Cuba. As he travelled God spoke to him: "You reach people by radio in the United States, why don't you do the same here in Cuba."

And so his radio program was translated into Spanish and listened to across Cuba, the Caribbean and down into South America. By 1955 the radio station was on 17 Latin American stations and 18 American ones. The work was still growing.

CHAPTER 14

TO THE GLORY OF GOD

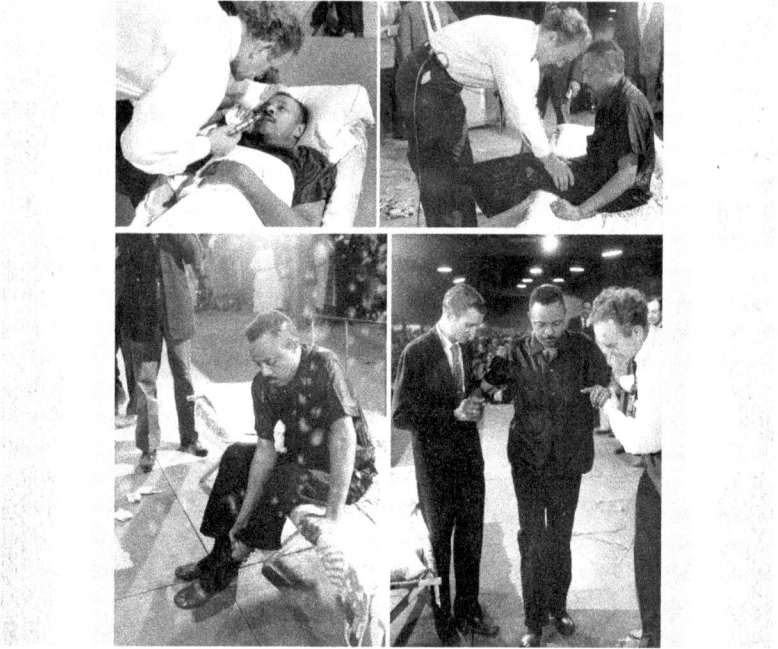

A man starts to walk after prayer

GOD IS REAL

So many people mock God. They don't believe he is there. Or if they do believe in him, they don't believe he can do anything to help them. God wants every single person to know about him. He loves people so much that he will do anything for them to see that he is God. He even sent his own son to die for us—that's how much God loves us!

There are some people who will never believe in God. Jesus said even if someone came back from the dead in front of them they would not believe in God. They know that if they believe in God then he will be in charge of their lives. They want to stay as god of their life. They don't want to give that up for God. If you talk to them they simply mock you.

But most people are waiting. They are waiting for someone to show them that God is real. If God is real, and we really are his followers, then miracles should follow us. After all Mark 16 tells us some of the signs that follow people who believe in God.

Miracles are great gifts from God because they point people to God. It's great when someone is healed because they are no longer in pain and suffering, but that's not the only reason God heals people. He wants people to see that he is real.

As we tell people about Jesus, God calls us not just to talk about Him, but to show Him to people by our love, by our lives and by His supernatural power. When people saw God working through Asa they could all see that God was alive and well and ready to help them. That's why thousands were saved in his meetings.

AMBULANCE MEN AMAZED

One man was brought to the miracle meetings by ambulance.

He was dying from lymphoma. He was so weak he could not even move. The doctors knew that it would not be long before he was dead.

The man did not want to die. He wanted to live. So he got the ambulance men to carry him into the service.

As Asa started to pray for him, the man felt strength flow through his body. By the time Asa had finished praying the man was jumping up from his bed and walking away.

The ambulance men could not believe it. When they brought him to the meeting he could not even sit up. When they took him home he sat in the front of the ambulance chatting to them the whole way home. He was perfectly healed.

BRAVE BOY BLEEDING

Little Timmie Dodge was just five years old. For two months now, he had bruises all over his body. His parents had 10 other children and none of them had needed a doctor before. They didn't think it could be serious. After all lots of boys get bruises as they play around.

Then Timmie started to bleed. Blood came out of his mouth and his nose. And it did not stop. Blood poured out for two hours at a time. Timmie's whole face went whiter and whiter as the blood left his body. His parents now knew something was seriously wrong.

That night he bled for four hours straight. Timmie needed a doctor. "Your child has thrombocytopenia. His blood can't clot," the doctor said. "Usually we can help people like this, but your son is too weak. He is going to die."

Timmie's parents were devastated. "Please give Timmie to me and I will look after him in the hospital," the doctor said. He was trying to be kind, but they needed more than kindness. They needed a miracle.

Rushing home they quickly found out where Asa was preaching. He was 1,800 miles. The whole family jumped into the car and started driving to him. As they drove Timmie started to bleed again.

"He needs a blood transfusion, or he is not going to make it to the meeting." his parents said. Let's stop and see another doctor. The other doctor could not help them.

"There is nothing that can be done to help him. Give him to me and I will look after him in the hospital until he dies."

The family did not want to give up on Timmie yet. They wanted God to save him. With 250 miles to go Timmie began bleeding once more. His whole body went pale and he almost passed out. But they kept going.

When they arrived he was still alive. They carried Timmie out of the car and burst into the tent. There was no meeting going on at that time. Asa was just about to leave. He prayed for Timmie and the bleeding stopped.

Timmie and his family were ready when the afternoon meeting began. He had bled so much that he was too weak to move. "Bring him onto the platform," Asa called. "We will pray for Timmie."

His small five year old body was easy to carry. Timmie's body seemed stiff as they carried him up. The whole congregation prayed for him. Three minutes later he sat up and spoke. "Please can I have an orange?"

Someone found an orange and Timmie ate it up! That night he was back in the meeting, sitting up and looking well. His parents stayed at the revival for the next few weeks. Timmie had been healed and they wanted everyone to see it.

Each night Asa looked over at Timmie. Soon his white face was a nice rosy pink color. A few days after he had been prayed for they took him to some doctors. They knew God had healed him, now they wanted the medical proof.

When the doctors had finished all their tests they smiled. "We can tell he did have thrombocytopenia, but there is no trace of it or any other illness in his body. It can only have been God that healed him."

CREATIVE MIRACLES

Mrs. Liscomb could hardly breathe. She had had TB and the doctors had found that one of her lungs had been destroyed. It was completely missing. The other lung was very badly damaged. Whenever she walked she had to stop every two steps to get her breath back. She could not do any work. She could not even bend down to pick up a piece of paper.

When she arrived at the tent, people had to help her fill in the card for healing. She was so out of breath. The stewards sat her in the emergency section and she waited. As people came forward to be prayed for, Mrs. Liscomb stood to pray for others. When she did she realized she could breathe. She did not have to fight for each breath. Her lungs were clear. BOTH her lungs were normal.

"I'm healed! Thank you, Jesus."

Mrs. Liscomb told everyone what God had done for her. Then she showed them by running around the tent. The lady who came in with half a lung left with two.

SUPERNATURAL SIGNS

But it wasn't just healings and salvations. God did lots of other miracles. Asa knew God could do miracles. Jesus fed 5000 people from one packed lunch and walked on the water. Jesus is still alive today and working through the church. Asa had seen God do miracles for himself. One time when he needed $300 God had turned $1 bills in his wallet into $20 bills. He wanted everyone else to know God is real.

Mrs. Alvester Williams was obese. As she sat in a healing service people watched her shrink. That night she lost 200 pounds in one go! That's the weight of a normal person. God had done a strange miracle in front of everyone.

In some meetings oil appeared on people's hand. Male and female, people from every race, children and adults all found oil on their hands. God was showing people that he could use anyone, not just the people who stood on a platform.

One evening a camera man was filming the oil that had appeared on his hands. As Asa lifted up one hand the camera man saw a bloody nail mark on the man's hand. Asa saw it too but God told him not to say anything for a few minutes. When he called for the man, the man had gone. The people had seen him, but he had completely disappeared.

They watched the film from the camera. It showed the man's hands, but the person's face could not be seen. Could it be that Jesus himself had stood with them? It seemed that God was doing more and more through Asa and his team. At every meeting people were healed, saved and set free to live for Jesus. Now it was time for the next stage of growth in the ministry.

CHAPTER 15

MIRACLE VALLEY

Inside a tent crusade

WE NEED A BASE

As people listened to the radio and came to the crusades there was more and more work to do. People wrote letter after letter asking for prayer. Asa started a newsletter to tell people what God was doing. Soon thousands of people wanted a copy each month.

It was clear that Asa needed to have a base. He was travelling all over the place, but he needed a new center to work from. A rancher gave him 1250 acres of land and Asa bought another 1250. Asa renamed the whole area Miracle Valley.

In the 1960s Asa built a church to seat 4000. He also built homes for his staff of 211 people and their families. Miracle Valley became a center for training missionaries and from there radio and television outreach could spread across the globe. The A. A. Allen ministry was now established and ready for the next stage.

MIRACLES BY RADIO

Gloria Macias had had warts all over her face since she was 8 years old. She was used to people staring at her and laughing at her, but she wanted to be free. One day she was listening to Asa on the radio with her family. When the program ended they looked at her. Your face is smooth. Your warts have gone. God had healed her.

Oscar Park had been very sick. He had cancer. Without an operation he would die. But the operation was very serious. Oscar had lost a toe because of the cancer. Now doctors cut out some of his lung, three of his ribs and some of his breast bone. They wanted to cut out every trace of cancer from his body. The doctors had saved his life.

One evening Oscar sat listening to the radio. Asa was preaching. "Reach out to God. He can do anything!"

As Oscar sat there he thought about his body. "God, when I come to you I want my body to be whole. Please can you sort my body out?" As he prayed, he reached over to the radio and put his hand on it. At that moment his chest bone, ribs and lung grew back.

The next morning when Oscar woke up he looked down at his feet. Both feet had five toes on. A new toe had grown overnight. Even the toenail on the new toe was perfect! God had done an amazing miracle.

On January 13th, 1952 Oscar went back to the surgeon who had cut out the cancer. It was only three months ago that he had had the operation.

"Can you do another X-ray of my chest please?" Oscar asked the surgeon.

"Sure," the surgeon said. But when the X-ray came he was puzzled. "I've either got the wrong X-ray or the wrong patient!" He knew he had cut out three ribs. No ribs were missing from the X-ray he was holding, so he took another X-ray. It was the same as the first one. The lungs were complete, the breast bone was all there and no ribs were missing.

"But we cut these out," the surgeon said. "I don't understand. They are all back again!"

Oscar understood. God had done a miracle. Doctors also knew he had a toe missing. But they could not argue with him when he took his socks off and showed them that his toe had now grown back.

GOD HEALS CHILDREN

Sammy was ten years old. He had polio.

Since that time his whole body had become useless. He could not even lift his head up by himself. Instead he had to wear special braces to hold his head in place. He had more braces on his legs. And the rest of his body was covered in leather and metal so that he could be kept standing.

His body was so twisted that he had to wear the braces all day. He even had to wear them when he slept at night. Sammy loved life. He just wanted to be able to run and join in with the other children when they played. When Sammy heard that Asa was coming near his town he wanted to go.

"Please let me go, Mum. I've heard about Asa, but I want to see him for myself."

So on March 24, 1959 Sammy went with a family friend to the meeting. When Asa got there, Sammy was ready to be prayed for. Asa picked him up and put him on his knee. Then he prayed, "God, come heal this child. I command this body to be whole in the name of Jesus."

Sammy felt something strange happening. For the first time ever all the pain had left him. He knew God had healed him. Sammy took the braces off with help from his friend. They used a screwdriver and pliers to get rid of the special shoes and the leather and metal around his body. Sammy stood up straight and walked across the platform. The crowd cheered—God had done a miracle.

When Sammy walked into his house he held his head up high. "How are you doing that? Where are you braces?" his mum asked. "How are you even walking?" She knew it was impossible for Sammy to walk without help. But with God all things are possible.

CHAPTER 16

CAUGHT IN THE ACT

A. A. Allen's tent from above

HE'S A DRUNK

Rumors started to go round the country.

Asa Allen was the son of a drunk. Now Asa Allen was a drunk. People heard of his past and nodded their head, "Of course it must be hard for him. We all have our demons that we have to fight. This must be his battle."

Sometimes it can be really hard to know what is true. Many people didn't believe the rumors. They knew that the devil will do anything to try and stop people from serving God. If he can't do that he will try to stop people from listening to servants of God. They saw this as a plot to ruin Asa's reputation. Other people believed the rumors. One thing was certain—his enemies were happy to help spread the rumors.

In the middle of the 1950s Asa was holding a crusade in Knoxville, Tennessee. Some of the pastors wanted Asa to hold the meeting in their church buildings. They knew that Asa would give them 10% of the offerings if the meetings were held in their church. They had big plans as to how they could use the money.

But because he held the meetings in an auditorium 10% of the offerings would be given direct to the denomination. They would not get any of the money they had hoped for. Every night Asa would drive himself and a couple of his workers to the auditorium ready for the meeting. Each night he would stop off at a café to have a glass of milk.

One night he stopped off as usual. Kent Rogers was with him in the car. "Rog, that milk tasted funny," Asa said. Kent shrugged, "Maybe it was sour."

Asa got in the car and started driving, but he felt really dizzy. "I better let someone else drive," and he pulled the car over to the side. At that moment the police arrived. When they tested him they found alcohol in his blood.

Amazingly the media and the pastors who were against him turned up with the police. What were they doing there? How did they know that Asa was about to be stopped by the police? Someone must have told them what was going to happen. Which means someone must have known it was going to happen.

Someone must have put something in his drink. Allen was given a ticket. The next day the newspapers screamed out their headlines: "Evangelist Allen was arrested for driving while drunk."

I'M CALLED TO PREACH NOT FIGHT

Allen could have stopped to fight, but he felt that the pastors only wanted to stop him. He was not going to be stopped from doing what God wanted him to do. Instead he paid the fine and carried on preaching the Gospel.

Asa wasn't drunk. His friend, Robert W. Schambach was in the car with Asa that night. Robert had been with Asa all evening. Robert was there when the police arrested. Robert was very clear, "he has not been drinking all night. If he had done I would have seen him."

When the police arrested Asa that was the final straw. The Assemblies of God could not take it anymore. They asked Asa to stop preaching. "I'm not going to stop preaching the Gospel. Thousands of people are dying without Jesus. I'm not going to stop preaching just because of this little thing. If you won't let me preach then I will leave your denomination."

They did not change their mind. Asa left them. God kept blessing the ministry and it kept on growing.

In 1968 they received 216,000 letters a day from 90 countries. 9,000 people were ordained ministers by Asa's ministry. 340,000 copies of the miracle magazine were sent out each month. 58 radio stations and 43 television stations showed his weekly broadcasts. Asa had been to 24 cities in America and two in the Philippines that year. God was doing much through him.

All this came at a great cost.

PERSECUTION AND SEPARATION

"I don't imagine that people are persecuting me everywhere I go," Asa explained. "But what else can you call it? So many times people have tried to destroy my ministry and stop me from preaching. It is persecution."

Wherever he went it seemed like the newspapers would write against him. Governments tried to slow him down with extra paper work. They accused him of not paying enough tax. Local leaders tried to persuade radio and television stations to stop showing his programs.

But Asa kept on fighting. He did not give up.

He started to speak out against certain churches and he focused more on giving money to God as his ministry grew. Asa raised lots of money. Some people thought he loved money, they did not know that he put it all back into the ministry. He didn't even own miracle valley, it all belonged to the ministry.

Was he being pulled away from what God had called him to do? Or was this a new phase of his ministry?

In 1967 Asa and Lexie stopped living together. God was using Asa, but his marriage was falling apart. It was a sad day for those who followed his ministry. Something bigger was about to happen in Asa's life that would get the whole of the church and some of the world talking. Asa would never know how it would affect people on earth. By the time people heard about it he would be dead.

CHAPTER 17

THE LAST DAYS OF HIS LIFE

A. A. Allen waves goodbye

TRAGEDY STRIKES

By 1969 Asa was not well. He had arthritis in his knee and was always in pain. Sometimes the pain was so bad that he asked others to take the meetings for him. Asa knew that he could not carry on like this. He went to the doctors and asked them to help him. When they suggested he should have an operation, Asa eventually agreed.

On June 11, 1970 Asa went to San Francisco. He had had one operation. He was going to see his doctor the next morning to see if he needed more surgery. Asa checked into his hotel around lunch time. He settled into his room. That evening he called a friend. Nobody knows what Asa said, but his friend was worried.

He rushed over to Asa's hotel. When he got there he spoke to the hotel manager. The manager got a spare key and they rushed up to Asa's room. When they walked in they found Asa sitting in front of the television. He was not breathing. That night, at 11:23 he was pronounced dead.

Strong medicines were scattered around the room. The coroner opened up Asa's body and did lots of tests. No drugs or medicine were in his blood. But he did have lots of alcohol. On his death certificate Asa died from a heart attack. Around his liver were fatty deposits caused by alcohol.

When you add this to the report of drink driving years earlier, it looks like Asa Allen died like his dad had—an alcoholic. It got everyone talking. "He had been an alcoholic when he was younger, it looks like he was never healed," some said.

"Is that why he didn't turn up to so many meetings in the last few years," other commented. "When you drink too much it makes you miss things you know."

"Did you know they found drugs all over his room? His friend Don Stewart cleaned them all up before anyone got there."

"He was only 59 years old. Just shows how dangerous alcohol is."

How do you think people felt? Many people had been saved as he preached the Gospel. Others had been healed. Now it seemed that the man who had helped them meet Jesus was an alcoholic.

But that's not the only version around.

THE LAST DAYS OF HIS LIFE (VERSION 2)

God had obviously used Asa loads in his life. Those closest to him said he never touched alcohol and he never smelt of it. They simply did not believe the reports.

In fact their version was very, very different.

We won't really know which is the true version, but a lot of things about the story of his death that you have just read didn't make sense to his friends. This is what they said happened.

Asa had been suffering from arthritis. His doctors had given him strong medicine to help with the pain. The doctor gave Asa very dangerous medicines to take. With these medicines you could end up needing more and more of them. Asa hated the medicines. They made him feel drowsy and stopped him from thinking clearly.

If you use these medicines with alcohol it is very dangerous. No doctor would give these medicines to someone who drank too much. Doctors are very good at telling who drinks too much. Alcoholics can hide their drink problem from their family sometimes, but not from their doctors. Even by looking at a person's hands they can tell if someone is drinking too much alcohol!

Asa had drunk lots as a child and a young adult. He had been brought up in a house full of alcohol. Now he used alcohol to take away the pain. Many other people used alcohol in the same way. In fact the doctors did not find the liver full of disease. Anyone who drinks lots of alcohol for a long time will start to kill their liver. Doctors call this cirrhosis. Asa's liver did not have cirrhosis.

Instead there were some fatty deposits around the liver. This is what happens when you drink lots of alcohol in a short period of time. When you stop drinking the fat goes away again.

So the doctors found that Asa had been drinking a lot for a short time. This agrees with Asa's friends' story—he had been using it to take away pain. We know he hadn't taken the medicines because when the coroner checked his blood he did not find any medicine there.

Asa was not an alcoholic; he was a man in a lot of pain. Asa was flying to see his doctor. He was desperate because he was in so much pain and he drank so much alcohol that he died. We don't know why God didn't heal his pain, but we do know that he was suffering.

IS SOMEONE TRYING TO SET HIM UP?

After he died lots of stories went around. Many people said that the room was full of empty bottles. But those who had found Asa did not find any bottles.

The story that Don Stewart had cleaned up drugs from his room surprised all his staff as they knew that Don was not in the same town as Asa. If he had been using other drugs the coroner would have found it in his blood. But he didn't.

When the friend went in with the hotel manager, they both found Asa together and called a doctor immediately.

How could any friend have cleaned up the room without the manager noticing?

In 1972, a couple of years after he had died a very strange thing happened. One lady was working in Miracle Valley. She was opening letters when out of one fell a check for $10,000. The check was not for the Allen ministry. It was for the person who had sent it.

The lady thought it must be a mistake until she read the letter.

"I was the coroner who examined Asa A. Allen after he died. I want to ask you to forgive me. I told lies to the media. I told them that he died from acute alcoholic poisoning which caused him to have liver damage. I am sending this check that was given to me to tell these lies. Please forgive me."

The check had been written by a group of churches who did not like Asa Allen. The lady gave the letter and the check to the directors. They read the letter and decided that one of them should go and meet the coroner. Before they could go to see him, the coroner was dead. He had killed himself.

Now they were not sure what to do. They got on well with the people from the other churches now. On Asa's death certificate it said he had a heart attack. They did not think the rumors of him drinking would carry on. So they decided not to do anything more about it.

Even today we still have these different stories about his death. Remember no one really knows what happened. The story from his friends seems to fit the facts we do know for sure. We know that men who serve God do mess up sometimes.

We also know that the enemy wants to shame men of God so that he can shame God. He loves to make up lies to make God's people look bad and so keep sinners away from God.

What we do know is that God used Asa in his life to lead many people to Jesus and to do great miracles.

ASA WAS A HUMAN BEING

Asa Allen made lots of mistakes in his life. But God still used him. God spoke to Asa and told him what he needed to do. But it took Asa years before he did it. Asa had a lot of fear, but he didn't let his fears stop him from serving God.

Near the end of his life he spent a lot of time talking about how bad other people were. Near the end of his life he was becoming bitter against other people. He should have put all of his energy into helping people meet with God instead of tearing people down. God calls us to love our enemies. At the end of his life Asa didn't seem to be doing that.

But we can learn from his successes and his mistakes. When God asks you to do something do it. Don't wait a week, act straight away. When you step out for God people will try and stop you and attack you. That's what they did to Asa. Jesus said this would happen to us in John 15:20: "Remember what I told you: 'A servant is not greater than his master.' If they persecuted me, they will persecute you also."

You don't need to worry about this. Instead we need to trust God. Almighty God knows what he is doing with our lives. Our job is to follow Him. If you make mistakes put your focus back on to God. Asa was not a superhuman. He was a human being just like Elijah and King David and the apostle Paul. He was a human being just like you.

If God can use all these people, God can use you too. He is just looking for people who are willing to pay the price to follow Him. When Asa paid the price, as God told him to, he started to see amazing miracles happen through his life. Many people were helped to find God and were set free to follow Him. God can use you to do supernatural things to help people know God.

Are you willing? What is God asking you to do today to follow him?

Don't worry about what has happened in the past, but decide to aim to follow God with all your heart today and into the future.

BIBLE STUDY FOR YOUNG GENERALS

Read Luke 6:39-40

1. If we follow someone who is not following God where will we end up (verse 39)?
2. Who is the teacher that we are following?
3. Write a long list of what Jesus is like (make sure these are not your own ideas but they are based on what the Bible tells us he is like)?
4. In what ways was Asa like Jesus?
5. In what ways would you like to become more like Jesus?
6. Think about how we can be trained to be more like him?

A. A. ALLEN
—ACTIVITY SECTION

REMEMBER THE BOOK

How much of the story can you remember? Test your memory by answering these questions.

Answers are given on page 118.

1. Where did Asa receive the gift of tongues?
2. What did Asa and Lexie do when, after two weeks of preaching, nobody was responding to the Gospel?
3. How many people were saved the next day?
4. How many things were on the list that God gave to Asa?
5. What did Asa do when he saw a boy whose shoes were falling apart?
6. What was Asa's book on healing called?

CHOOSE THE RIGHT ANSWER

Answers are given on page 118.

1. What was Asa's childhood like?

   A. Very happy

   B. Okay

   C. Awful

2. How quickly did Asa stop drinking and smoking after he met Jesus?

   A. Immediately

   B. After one month

   C. After a year

3. How old was Asa when he first ran away from home?

   A. 5

   B. 11

   C. 14

4. What happened in Asa's home on Saturday nights when he was a young man?

   A. Bible studies

   B. Parties

   C. He watched TV

5. In what year did Asa hold the first tent meeting?

    A. 1934

    B. 1945

    C. 1951

6. What did Asa use to tell people about what Jesus was doing?

    A. A newsletter

    B. The radio

    C. Television

ANSWERS

1. In a Pentecostal camp, 2. They stayed up all night to pray, 3. Twenty-three, .4. Thirteen, 5. He gave his son's only pair of shoes, 6. God's guarantee to heal you.

1. C, 2. A, 3. B, 4. B, 5. C, 6. A, B & C.

AROUND THE WORLD

A. A. Allen travelled around America a lot. Time yourself to find out how quickly can you find these places in America *in the order they are written.* Can you spot the one place that is not in America?

1. Arkansas
2. Idaho
3. Cuba
4. Texas

5. Arizona
6. California
7. Colorado
8. Tennessee

Write down your times here.

Date	Time Taken

PUZZLE IT

Find the names of all 12 people in the 'God's Generals for kids' series in the grid below. Their first name and family name will be near to each other. Choose a different color to color in each person's name. Have you read the whole series?

1. Kathryn Kuhlman
2. Smith Wigglesworth
3. John Dowie
4. Maria Woodworth-Etter
5. Evan Roberts
6. Charles Parham
7. William Seymour
8. John Lake
9. Aimee Semple McPherson
10. William Branham
11. Jack Coe
12. A. A. Allen

C	K	A	T	H	R	Y	N	M	A	R	I	A	W
H	U	W	L	J	O	H	N	C	E	T	U	I	O
A	H	I	S	L	A	K	E	P	L	O	O	M	O
R	L	G	K	O	N	L	Y	H	T	O	J	E	D
L	M	G	E	D	S	U	S	E	M	P	L	E	W
E	A	L	J	O	H	N	S	R	T	H	E	O	O
S	N	E	N	W	E	W	H	S	W	O	B	E	R
P	A	S	M	I	T	H	G	O	I	W	J	A	T
A	A	W	N	E	O	U	R	N	L	I	A	F	H
R	A	O	A	I	T	H	A	N	L	L	C	O	E
H	L	R	O	B	E	R	T	S	I	L	K	D	T
A	L	T	M	A	V	K	E	S	A	I	I	T	T
M	E	H	B	R	A	N	H	A	M	A	P	E	E
R	N	F	E	C	N	T	S	E	Y	M	O	U	R

When you have found all the names, write down the remaining letters below, reading from left to right. Start in the top left-hand corner of the grid.

Answer is given on page 124.

— — —   — —   — — — —   — — — —

— —   — — — — —   — — —   — — —

— — —   — — — — —   — — —

— — — —   — — —   — — — — —

— —   — — — — — — —. (Hebrews 12:2)

FIND IT OUT

Regrow leftovers. When it feels like we have nothing but rubbish left in our life, God can turn it into something good. See if you can use these leftovers to grow new plants.

1. Green Onions

Cut the green onion to leave around 2 inches by the white root base (you can use what you cut off in your food). Place the root base in a glass with enough water to completely cover the base and place it on a sunny windowsill. Cut off what you need as they'll grow back fast.

2. Celery

Chop off the base of the celery and rinse it in water. Place the base in a bowl of warm water on a sunny windowsill. Change the water every couple of days and keep the top of the base moist. Leaves will start to grow in the middle of the plant.

3. Basil

Take a few stems from a basil plant. They should be around 4 inches long. Remove all the leaves from the stem except for the ones at the top of the stem. Put the stems in a glass of water and place in a sunny spot. Change the water every other day. Roots will form after a few days. Once the roots start to grow, transfer the plants to some soil and watch them grow.

4. Garlic

Take one clove of garlic into a container full of soil. Bury the garlic to twice its depth. Water well and wait.

ANSWER TO PUZZLE IT

Let us look only to Jesus, the One who began our faith and makes it perfect. (Hebrews 12:2)

QUESTIONS TO THINK ABOUT

1. What were the differences between the way the different plants grew?
2. What did all the plants need to grow?
3. What do we need to grow spiritually?

FOR FURTHER RESEARCH

Find out what other vegetables you can grow from scraps.

YOUR TURN

Hebrews 12:1 tells us that, because we are surrounded by people who have lived their lives fully for God, we should do the same.

Who has encouraged you to live fully for God?

1. People from the Bible. (You can read about some of these people in Hebrews 11).
2. People from the God's Generals for Kids series.

3. Members of your family or church.

4. Other people whose stories encourage you to follow God more.

Get hold of photos or pictures for each of these people and create a picture collage out of them. Put the collage up in your room to encourage you to keep living for Jesus.

GET CREATIVE

Imagine you are A. A. Allen and you are about to hold a crusade in a town that you have never been to before. Create a poster to put up around the town to tell people that you are coming and what you are expecting God to do.

AUTHORS' NOTE TO READERS AND PARENTS

Like A. A. Allen, I believe that God can cure people miraculously today. I do not believe that this is the only way that God will work. God gives wisdom and knowledge to us to help us fight disease. Medicine continues to advance and medical care can actually be part of God's plan for bringing relief and healing to His people. However, medicine still does not hold all the answers. I am in favor of both competent medical treatment and the power of prayer. I would not encourage anyone to neglect either of these at their time of need.

BIBLIOGRAPHY

Asa A. Allen, *The Price Of God's Miracle Working Power* (Public Domain)

Asa A. Allen, Miracle Magazine: Various editions of magazine (Dallas, TX: A. A. Allen Revivals inc, 1955-1958 and Hereford, AZ: A. A. Allen Revivals inc, 1958-1965)

Paul Asa Allen, *In The Shadow Of Greatness: Growing Up "Allen"* (Tuscon, AZ: Paul Asa Allen, 2008)

John W. Carver, *The Life And Ministry Of A. A. Allen as Told By A. A. & Lexie Allen* (Westminster, MD: Faith Outreach International Publishing 2010)

David Edwin Harrell Jr., *All Things Are Possible: The Healings And Charismatic Revivals In Modern America* (Bloomington, IN: Indiana University Press 1978)

Roberts Liardon, *God's Generals: Why They Succeeded And Why Some Failed* (Tulsa, OK: Whitaker House 1996)

AUTHORS' CONTACT INFORMATION

ROBERTS LIARDON

Roberts Liardon Ministries, United States office:
P.O. Box 781888, Orlando, FL 32878
E-mail: Info1@robertsliardon.org
www.robertsliardon.org

United Kingdom/European office:
Roberts Liardon Ministries
22 Notting Hill Gate, Suite 125
London W11 3JE, UK

OLLY GOLDENBERG

BM Children Can, London WC1N 3XX, UK
info@childrencan.co.uk
www.childrencan.co.uk

ALSO AVAILABLE FROM BRIDGE-LOGOS

GOD'S GENERALS FOR KIDS (SERIES)
Roberts Liardon & Olly Goldenberg

This series has been growing in popularity and it focusses on the lives and teachings of great Christian leaders from times past. These books are written for children between the ages of eight and twelve. Newly released and enhanced, each book now includes an updated study section with cross curricular themes, suitable for home schooling groups. Kathryn Kuhlman (Vol. 1), and Smith Wigglesworth (Vol. 2) begin the series. Also available: John Alexander Dowie, Maria Woodworth-Etter, Evan Roberts, Charles Parham, William Seymour, John G. Lake, Aimee Semple McPherson, William Branham, Jack Coe and A.A. Allen.

GOD'S GENERALS FOR KIDS

12 VOLUMES TO COLLECT

BY ROBERTS LIARDON & OLLY GOLDENBERG

BRIDGE LOGOS

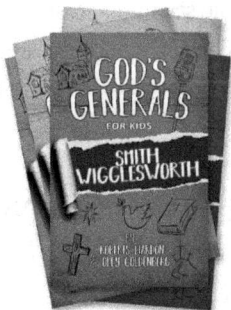

EVIDENCE BIBLE
Ray Comfort

Apologetic answers to over 200 questions, thousands of comments, and over 130 informative articles will help you better comprehend and share the Christian faith.

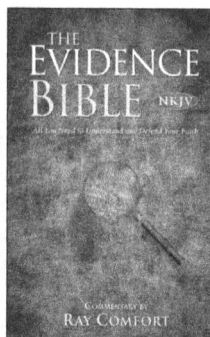

ISBN: 9780882705255

SCIENTIFIC FACTS IN THE BIBLE
Ray Comfort

Most people, even Christians, don't know that the Bible contains a wealth of incredible scientific, medical, and prophetic facts. That being so, the implications are mind boggling.

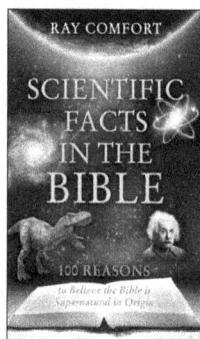

ISBN: 9780882708799

HOW TO KNOW GOD EXISTS
Ray Comfort

Does God exist, or does He not? In this compelling book, Ray Comfort argues the case with simple logic and common sense. This book will convince you that belief in God is reasonable and rational—a matter of fact and not faith.

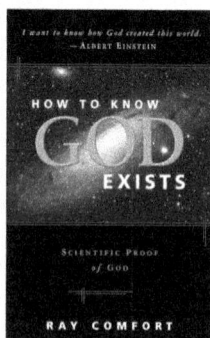

ISBN: 9780882704326

SCHOOL OF BIBLICAL EVANGELISM
Ray Comfort & Kirk Cameron

This comprehensive study offers 101 lessons on thought-provoking topics including basic Christian doctrines, cults and other religions, creation/evolution, and more. Learn how to share your faith simply, effectively, and biblically... the way Jesus did.

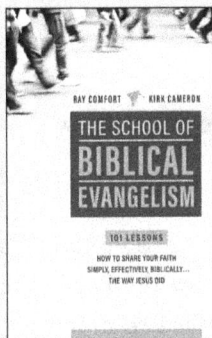

ISBN: 9780882709680

WAY OF THE MASTER STUDENT EDITION
Ray Comfort & Allen Atzbi

Youth today are being inundated with opposing messages, and desperately need to hear the truth of the gospel. How can you reach them? Sharing the good news is much easier than you think... by using some timeless principles.

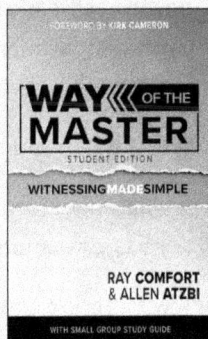

ISBN: 9781610364737

BRIDGE LOGOS

FOR A COMPLETE LIST OF BOOKS, TRACTS, AND VIDEOS BY RAY COMFORT, SEE

LIVINGWATERS.COM

ALSO AVAILABLE FROM BRIDGE-LOGOS

BEAUTY FROM ASHES
Donna Sparks

In a transparent and powerful manner, the author reveals how the Lord took her from the ashes of a life devastated by failed relationships and destructive behavior to bring her into a beautiful and powerful relationship with Him. The author encourages others to allow the Lord to do the same for them.

Donna Sparks is an Assemblies of God evangelist who travels widely to speak at women's conferences and retreats. She lives in Tennessee.

www.story-of-grace.com

www.facebook.com/
  donnasparksministries/

www.facebook.com/
  AuthorDonnaSparks/

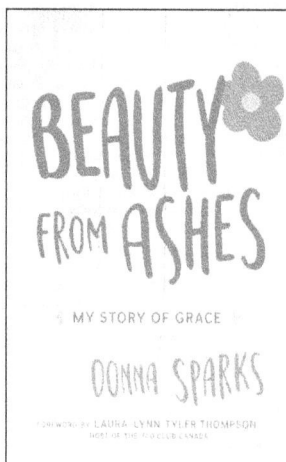

BEAUTY FROM ASHES

MY STORY OF GRACE

DONNA SPARKS

FOREWORD BY LAURA LYNN TYLER THOMPSON

ISBN: 978-1-61036-252-8

BRIDGE
LOGOS

ALSO AVAILABLE FROM BRIDGE-LOGOS

ALL THE WILD PEARLS
Heather DeJesus Yates

Every pearl has a story to tell. Join lawyer, speaker and author Heather DeJesus Yates as she creatively guides our generation through the transformational hope of the Gospel using both her own redemptive stories and those of an unlikely companion...a wild oyster.

Heather DeJesus Yates is a wife, mama, business owner, speaker, blogger, occasional lawyer and legislative advocate, and author. Out of a passion to see women walk in freedom from shame, Heather woos women into God's wide love through her disarmingly real-life stories, balanced with Gospel-centered hope.

Facebook: @amotherofthousands
Instagram: @amotherofthousands
Pinterest: @amotherofthousands.
www.facebook.com/amotherofthousands
www.amotherofthousands.com

ISBN: 978-1-61036-991-6

BRIDGE LOGOS

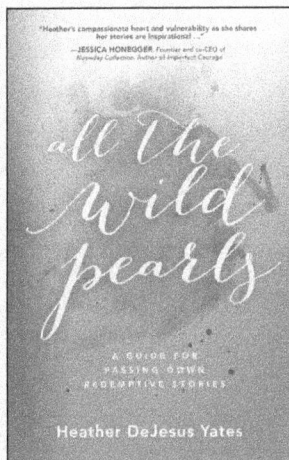

ALSO AVAILABLE FROM BRIDGE-LOGOS

OUR GOOD FATHER
Pierre M. Eade

Jesus said, "No one knows the Son except the Father, and no one knows the Father except the Son". He went on to give one exception, "and those to whom the Son chooses to reveal him."

If you desire a revelation of God the Father, you only have one place you need to go, listen to his son Jesus. Our Good Father takes the words of Jesus to bring a fresh understanding to the person of God the Father. Through the use of personal stories, analogies and humor, Our Good Father uses the words of Jesus to paint a picture of the true nature of God.

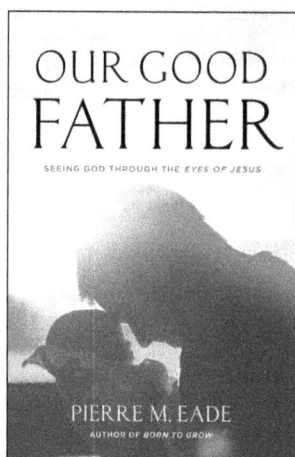

OUR GOOD
FATHER

SEEING GOD THROUGH THE *EYES OF JESUS*

PIERRE M. EADE
AUTHOR OF *BORN TO GROW*

ISBN: 9781610361774

BRIDGE
LOGOS

www.ingramcontent.com/pod-product-compliance
Lightning Source LLC
Chambersburg PA
CBHW070826100426
42813CB00003B/501